LIVING LIKE JESUS

Jesus' teaching for everyday life

TIM MAYFIELD
with James Jones

Illustrations by Taffy

 the bible reading fellowship

Text copyright Tim Mayfield © 1993
Illustrations copyright Taffy © 1993

The author asserts the moral right
to be identified as the author of this work

Published by
The Bible Reading Fellowship
Peter's Way
Sandy Lane West
Oxford
OX4 5HG
ISBN 0 7459 2529 4
Albatross Books Pty Ltd
PO Box 320
Sutherland
NSW 2232
Australia
ISBN 0 7324 0660 9

First edition 1993

Acknowledgments
Scripture quotations are taken from *The Holy Bible, New
International Version*: copyright © New York International Bible
Society, 1978, and published by Hodder & Stoughton Ltd.

A catalogue record for this book is available
from the British Library

Printed and bound in Slovenia

Contents

A word in your ear . . .   4

Section One: Counting the Cost   5
1   Build on the rock—*Matthew 7:24–27*   6
2   Living against the flow—*Matthew 7:13–14*   8
3   Count the cost!—*Luke 14:28–30*   10
4   The flavour of God—*Matthew 5:13*   12
5   Come and rest—*Matthew 11:28–30*   14
    Headline 1   16

Section Two: Love and Service   17
6   Desert Island Discs—*Mark 12:29–31*   18
7   The golden rule—*Matthew 7:12*   20
8   Show your love—*John 13:3–5*   22
9   Love your enemy—*Luke 6:32–35*   24
10 The extra mile—*Matthew 5:38–42*   26
11 Pray for healing—*Luke 9:1–2, 6*   28
12 Stick at it!—*Luke 18:1–8*   30
    Headlines 1–2   32

Section Three: Changing the World   33
13 God's yeast—*Matthew 13:33*   34
14 Rich man, poor man—*Luke 16:19–21*   36
15 You did it for me—*Matthew 25:34–40*   38
16 Set them free!—*Luke 4:18–19*   40
17 The Christian and politics—*Matthew 22:18–22*   42
    Headlines 1–3   44

Section Four: Inside Out   45
18 Whitewashed tombs—*Matthew 23:25–28*   46
19 Be reconciled!—*Matthew 5:23–24*   48

20 Mind the plank!—*Matthew 7:3–5*   50
21 Father, forgive them!—*Matthew 18:21–22*   52
22 The adultery of the heart—*Matthew 5:27–28*   54
23 The overflow—*Matthew 12:34–37*   56
    Headlines 1–4   58

Section Five: Your Money and Your Life   59
24 Give generously—*Luke 6:38*   60
25 Secret giving—*Matthew 6:2–4*   62
26 The rich fool—*Luke 12:16–21*   64
27 Treasure in heaven—*Matthew 6:19–21*   66
28 Give to the poor—*Mark 10:17–22*   68
29 Don't worry!—*Luke 12:22–26*   70
    Headlines 1–5   72

Section Six: Power for Living   73
30 Coming home—*Luke 15:20–24*   74
31 The secret place—*Matthew 6:6–8*   76
32 Stay in the city—*Luke 24:49; Acts 1:5*   78
33 Come and drink—*John 7:37–39*   80
34 Remain in the vine—*John 15:5–8*   82
    Headlines 1–6   84

Section Seven: Stake Your All   85
35 Keep watch!—*Luke 12:35–40*   86
36 Stake your all!—*Matthew 13:44–46*   88
37 Send the invitation—*Luke 14:16–23*   90
    Headlines 1–7   92

Group study material   93

A word in your ear...

I wrote this book because I **want** to live like Jesus, not because I already do. Through it, I want God to change me ... and you as well. I want us both to become more like Jesus than we are now.

Why?

Because the life of Jesus was a masterpiece. Here is a man of love: always quick to see the needs of others. Here is a man of courage: able to hear God's call and respond with all his heart. Here is a man of justice, who hurts for the poor. Here is a man of truth: able to say what needs saying, however uncomfortable.

You and I need to hear those words of truth. And we can, because this Jesus is alive today. He has promised to help us live like him. I pray he will use this book to do that.

You could work through the book on your own. You could work through it with your Bible study group (hints for how to use the book in groups are on page 93). However you use it, be as honest with yourself and with God as you can. You'll grow as a result.

Section One: Counting the Cost

Putting the teaching of Jesus into practice is like building on solid rock (unit 1). But those who do so are in a small minority, living against the flow (2). So a follower of Jesus should count the cost of belonging to him (3) and be the flavour of God in the world (4). He or she should bear in mind that following Jesus can be taxing, and find enough time to rest (5).

1 *Build on the rock*

We built a splendid family sandcastle at Whitby. It had everything: towers, moats, bridges and tunnels. But when the tide came in we had to retreat to the pier. We watched the castle crumble and dissolve. In the morning all that remained was a flat stretch of wet sand.

For a very different kind of castle, go to Edinburgh. Stand on Princes Street and take it all in. The huge rock foundation. The massive battlements. Try and work out a way of storming the place. And then think better of it!

There's a world·of difference between sand and rock. That's why Jesus chose those two substances to underline the effect of his teaching . . .

Read:

> *Everyone who hears these words of mine and puts them into practice is like a*
> *wise man who built his house on the rock. The rain came down, the streams*
> *rose, and the winds blew and beat against that house; yet it did not fall,*
> *because it had its foundation on the rock. But everyone who hears these words*
> *of mine and does not put them into practice is like a foolish man who built*
> *his house on sand. The rain came down, the streams rose, and the winds blew*
> *and beat against that house, and it fell with a great crash.*

Matthew 7:24–27

According to Jesus, the best foundation you can have for living is to listen to his teaching and put it into practice. This book aims to help you do that. We'll read the Master's words, think about what they mean today, and take steps to live them out. Then together we'll build our lives on a rock that'll never let us down: on Jesus—the Rock of Ages.

Put each of the qualities listed below in the 'rock' column or the 'sand' column . . .

Rock		Sand
	Unreliable Solid Dependable Soft Strong Shifting Unstable Durable	

Now tick the box which most sums you up . . .

☐ *I'd like to follow Jesus and build my life on the rock.*

☐ *I'd prefer to go it alone and work it out for myself.*

Pray:

Father, help me to hear what Jesus is saying to me.
Help me to understand what it means for today.
And please help me to live it out. Amen.

HAVE YOU GOT PLANNING PERMISSION !?

2 | *Living against the flow*

My brother and I squeezed onto the packed train. It was heading from Manchester Piccadilly to Old Trafford, the home of Manchester United. The journey was an uncomfortable one. Everyone else on board wore the red and white of the home team. Only my brother and I wore the blue and white of visitors West Brom.

Foolish? Heroic? Who knows. But it sticks in my mind as a memory of being different. Of being looked at, whispered about, 'Not one of us'.

That feeling of standing out in a crowd will be shared by anyone who whole-heartedly decides to follow Jesus. The master himself tells us as much...

Read:

> *Enter through the narrow gate. For wide is the gate and broad is the road that leads to destruction, and many enter through it. But small is the gate, and narrow the road that leads to life, and only a few find it.*
>
> **Matthew 7:13–14**

From the beginning, Jesus was aware that only a few would squeeze through the narrow gate to life. The rest by-pass it. They prefer to stick together on the wide and easy road. No wonder the Christian life can feel a lonely business at times. We're living against the flow, called to be different from those around us. That's why it's always taken courage to be a Christian. But take heart! You're in good company. Go for it!

WE'RE STICKING OUT
LIKE SORE THUMBS

Here's a list of areas where Christians are called to be 'different' from those around them. Shade the bar to the extent that you think you are different...

As a Christian, I'm called to be different in my attitudes to:

Race	
Gossip	
Money	
Promotion	
Honesty	
The Third World	

Now look at the bar you shaded least. What one thing could you do today to make it longer?

Pray:

*Father God, it **is** lonely sometimes, and difficult.*
But this narrow road you've put me on leads to life.
With your help, I'll walk it all the way. Thank you God. Amen.

3 | *Count the cost!*

Near where I live, some brave families have built their own houses. They lived across the road in caravans until the work was finished. Then one by one the houses were completed and the caravans towed away.

But what if one of the builders had run out of cash half-way through? If he'd started the project confident he could finish but then had run out of funds? He'd be forced to live in a caravan opposite the empty shell of his dream house.

Jesus told a story like that to warn us about the cost of following him:

Read:

> *Suppose one of you wants to build a tower. Will he not first sit down and estimate the cost to see if he has enough money to complete it? For if he lays the foundation and is not able to finish it, everyone who sees it will ridicule him, saying, 'This fellow began to build and was not able to finish.'*
>
> **Luke 14:28–30**

Living the Christian life is often hard. That's why Jesus warns us to **count the cost** before we follow him. He wants whole-hearted disciples. People who have spotted some of the difficulties but still say 'yes, Jesus! I'll follow you. Lead on! I'll go wherever you take me.'

Here are some common difficulties people face in following Jesus. Take time to consider each one. If you face it now, tick the first column. If you fear it in the future, tick the second...

	Now	Future
Mockery at work		
The cold shoulder from friends		
Misunderstanding from family		
A change in my habits with money		
A change in my habits with sex		
Greater honesty		

Pray:

Well, Jesus, I've counted the cost, and it's worth paying. You give me the kind of life I can find nowhere else. So I'm glad to follow you. Give me courage and strength. And let my life bring honour to you. Amen.

TO BE CONTINUED WHEN MORE MONEY ARRIVES

4 | *The flavour of God*

One morning a complete disaster struck our family. I forgot to put salt in the porridge. After half an hour spent lovingly preparing it I was desperate to tuck in. But it was a major disappointment: flat, lifeless, and watery. No salt.

The following day I was determined not to repeat the mistake. So pouring a tiny pile of salt into my palm I stirred it in. The result: perfection! The salt had woken up my taste buds. The whole dish jumped to life.

Jesus had that effect in mind when he told his disciples . . .

Read:

You are the salt of the earth. But if the salt loses its saltiness, how can it be made salty again? It is no longer good for anything, except to be thrown out and trampled by men.

Matthew 5:13

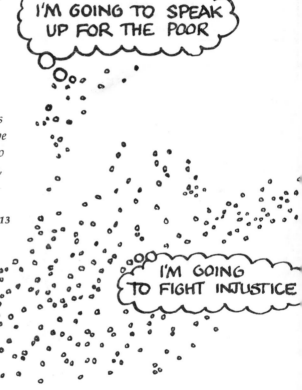

I'M GOING TO SPEAK UP FOR THE POOR

I'M GOING TO FIGHT INJUSTICE

In Jesus' mind we're to have the same effect on the world as that salt in my porridge. We're to work through the whole dish . . . and bring the flavour of God to a society gone stale and fl[a]

A tall order? Maybe. But even a handful of full-flavour Christians can have an amazing effect. Try it sometime!

I WONDER WHERE I'M HEADED?

Jesus calls us to take the flavour of God with us wherever we go. But what flavour is he? In this word square are ten tastes of God. Try and find them...

Q	C	Z	B	W	O	L	N	F	T	S
R	E	C	I	T	S	U	J	G	S	D
N	L	O	F	J	H	B	Y	E	R	H
P	E	G	L	A	N	T	N	N	O	V
A	B	S	E	O	P	E	U	E	C	H
C	R	R	M	L	V	N	W	R	P	D
S	A	T	P	I	L	E	D	O	T	R
C	T	R	G	F	S	H	C	S	E	A
Y	I	R	V	E	D	B	Q	I	B	P
S	O	T	S	Y	M	P	A	T	H	Y
F	N	J	A	B	G	C	F	Y	M	C

Joy
Life
Forgiveness
Love
Generosity
Care
Sympathy
Justice
Truth
Celebration

Now write three places outside the church where you will spend time this week. Alongside each one, write which particular flavour of God, from the list above, that place needs most.

	Place	*Flavour*
1.		
2.		
3.		

Pray:

Father, help me when I go into the places I've listed. Help me to live for you, and spread your flavour through me. Amen.

5 Come and rest

If you go for a long drive, there will come a time when you have to take on more petrol. If you don't, you'll end up out of fuel, on the hard shoulder, and in a big mess.

If you run a cassette player from batteries, there will come a time when you have to recharge them. If you don't, the thing could grind to a halt in the middle of your favourite track.

Refuelling, recharging, call it what you like: human beings have to do it too. Otherwise we end up drained of energy. Worse still, our bodies, or even our minds, might protest at the overload.

We need to **rest**. That's why the Sabbath day was so important in the Old Testament. And that's why Jesus offers us his great invitation in Matthew's Gospel...

Read:

Come to me, all you who are weary and burdened, and I will give you rest. Take my yoke upon you and learn from me, for I am gentle and humble in heart, and you will find rest for your souls. For my yoke is easy and my burden is light.

Matthew 11:28–30

In the church, it's easy to become *weary and burdened*. There's so much to do, and well-meaning people ask us to take on responsibilities. We need to be careful. We need to say 'yes' to what we feel called to—and do it with the best of our ability. We need to say 'no' to what we are not called to, and not feel guilty. And we need to make sure that there's enough time in our lives simply to rest.

■ **To help you do that, fill in this questionnaire...**

Do I have enough time to rest?   Yes/No
When I'm asked to do a job, do I ever say 'no'?   Yes/No
When I take on a new job I always lay down an old one. True/False

List here jobs that you do that you feel called to:

> 1.

List here jobs that you do not feel called to but do out of a sense of duty, or because you've never thought of giving up:

> 2.

Now looking at box 2, list here jobs that you could, in time, pass on to somebody else:

> 3.

Pray:

Jesus, thank you that you don't want me to become weary and burdened. Thank you that you call me to rest. Help me to find time to recharge my batteries, and time when I can come to you and rest. Amen.

Headline

Look back through Section One. What **one thing** would you like to work on to help you **live like Jesus**? Write it in one sentence in this box . . .

1.

Section Two: Love and Service

To Jesus, love is the most important thing of all (unit 6). Love means treating other people as we like to be treated (7) and is something we **do**, not just something we **say** (8). Jesus calls us to love our enemies (9) which is like carrying a soldier's pack further than we need to (10). Love involves praying for healing (11) and sticking at it through discouragement (12).

6 | *Desert Island Discs*

On Desert Island Discs a celebrity imagines they're about to be marooned on an island. They can take eight records with them. As they describe their choice of music the listeners find out what's really important to that person.

Something a bit like that once happened to Jesus. Someone came up and asked him to think about the whole Old Testament. Out of all the hundreds of rules, which was the most important? Jesus' reply tells us something very important about **him** . . .

Read:

> *The most important one . . . is this: 'Hear, O Israel, the Lord our God, the Lord is one. Love the Lord your God with all your heart and with all your soul and with all your mind and with all your strength.' The second is this: 'Love your neighbour as yourself.' There is no commandment greater than these.*
>
> **Mark 12:29–31**

To Jesus, one word sums up what it's all about: **love**. Being a Christian isn't about keeping hundreds of rules. It's about being in love with God. It's about receiving his love and returning it. It's about showing that love in action. That's the Christian life. A great adventure of love.

IF YOU WERE STUCK ON A DESERT ISLAND WHICH EIGHT COMMANDMENTS WOULD YOU TAKE WITH YOU?

Here's a list of things about love. Choose the three that are most important for you...

Love means . . .

... *always hoping the best for someone*

... *enjoying someone's company*

... *telling someone how much they mean to you*

... *forgiving and forgetting*

... *serving other people*

... *protecting and providing*

... *putting yourself second*

... *never giving up on somebody*

... *feeding the starving*

... *understanding other people's faults*

Now look at the list and the circle the one you're least good at. Then ask God to help you love like that...

Pray:

Lord, thank you that your love for me is perfect. Thank you that I'm special to you. Please help me to return the love you have for me. And to reflect it better in my dealings with others. Amen.

7 | *The golden rule*

Once upon a time the Jewish Rabbi Hillel was asked to quote the whole Old Testament standing on one leg. So he casually lifted one foot off the ground and said 'Do not do to your neighbour what is hateful to you. That is the whole law and the rest is commentary.'

Not a bad answer, I suppose. But it's all a bit negative. It consists of **not** doing things—of avoiding what would hurt those around me.

For the Master, of course, that is not enough. True life doesn't come by **avoiding** things! True life comes through **action**! Through thinking what is best for our neighbour and then doing it ...

Read:

In everything, do to others what you would have them do to you, for this sums up the Law and the Prophets.

Matthew 7:12

Those words form another of Jesus' definitions of that word 'love'. 'Love' means to put yourself in somebody else's shoes. Then to think 'if I were this person, what would I need?' And then to give it to them. This is discipleship! Live it to the full!

In the box below, write five ways in which you need to be treated, for example, 'I need people to listen to me'. Then alongside each one, in the smaller box, score yourself out of 10 for how much you do those things to others...

1.	
2.	
3.	
4.	
5.	

Which one did you give yourself the lowest mark for? What do you need to do to make it higher? Write it in this box...

Pray:

Lord Jesus, I'm sorry that sometimes I get so lost in my own needs that I can't see the needs of others. Help me to change. Give me a quick eye to see what others need, and to meet it with a generous spirit. Amen.

8 *Show your love*

I once spent a summer holiday hiking across Dartmoor. After about fifteen miles your feet get very hot and tired. So it was brilliant to chance across a moorland stream and kick off your boots. To plunge your feet into cool, fresh water was amazing ... fantastic ... a taste of heaven.

The Middle East is hotter and dustier than Dartmoor, of course. Feet easily become dusty and tired. After a long journey it's a lovely thing to bathe those feet and refresh them. But in Jesus' day washing someone else's feet was a very lowly task. Not even a slave was forced to wash his master's feet. Yet Jesus did this for his friends. On the night before he died ...

Read:

> *Jesus knew that ... he had come from God and was returning to God; so he got up from the meal, took off his outer clothing, and wrapped a towel round his waist. After that he poured water into a basin and began to wash his disciples' feet, drying them with the towel that was wrapped round him.*
>
> **John 13:3–5**

By washing their feet, Jesus **showed** his disciples **the full extent of his love**. It was a lovely action. He was not forced to do it. He just did, because their feet were tired and because he loved them. But there was a deeper meaning behind what he did. He wanted his disciples to follow his example. He knew it's no good simply **saying** that we love people. We've got to **show** that love in the things that we do.

☐ **Write here the Christian name of someone you love...**

Now write down something you can do today to *show your love* for that person.

Pray:

Lord Jesus, thank you that even as you faced death you were loving those around you. Help me to follow you. Help me to love others not only in my words, but also in my deeds. Amen.

OF COURSE I LOVE YOU — I GOT YOU THESE FLOWERS!

9 | *Love your enemy*

'Get out of my house, you!' The upper cut landed on my jaw. 'I'm sick to death of ruddy sky-pilots!' A well aimed kick hit my backside.

'Be careful, Geoff', I warned, 'that's assault!' With a vice-like grip he marched me up the drive. 'Just get off my land before I show you what assault really means!' He slung me onto the road.

I'd been called to that house before. Geoff and his wife were always fighting, and Geoff had seen sense in the past. Not on this occasion: I was forced to leave man and wife to their domestic bliss.

But Geoff and I were **neighbours**! How was I to react next time we met? I found these words of Jesus helpful:

Read:

If you love those who love you, what credit is that to you? Even 'sinners' love those who love them. And if you do good to those who are good to you, what credit is that to you? Even 'sinners' do that ... But love your enemies, do good to them, and lend to them without expecting to get anything back.

Luke 6:32–35

Those words don't mean I have to fall in love with Geoff. But they do call me honestly to want what is best for him.

This was put to the test a few days later. I was driving along when I saw Geoff struggling with his broken-down car. There was a tussle in my mind. But really the disciple of Jesus has no option. I stopped and helped him push it home.

◪ **So much for Geoff and myself. How about you? In this box, write the initials of someone you dislike ...**

Now ask yourself two questions ...

Do I really want what is best for that person?

What can I do today to put that into practice?

Make notes in the box provided ...

Pray:

Father, you know it's difficult sometimes.
There are people I find really impossible.
But you love those people perfectly. So help
me to love them too: to want what is best
for them, and to put that love into action.
Amen.

10 | *The extra mile*

AD31. July. Marcus dumped his heavy pack on the ground. Sitting on the milestone he wiped the beads of sweat from his forehead. Still five miles to Jerusalem. He cursed the day he'd been sent to this god-forsaken hole, and longed to see Italy again.

Then his eyes lit up. A young Jewish man was walking along the road towards him. Marcus spat on the ground and stood up. 'Hey you there! Jew! Carry my pack the next mile!'

The Jew's response amazed him. Without complaint he shouldered the heavy load, and they set off. The Roman soldier represented a hated occupying army. But you'd never have guessed it as the young Jew asked about his family back home, and when he'd see them again.

The next milepost came and went. Still the Jew struggled on with the heavy pack. Marcus was confused. This had never happened before! But the young man was only living out the revolutionary new teaching of Jesus . . .

Read:

You have heard that it was said, 'Eye for eye, and tooth for tooth.' But I tell you, Do not resist an evil person. If someone strikes you on the right cheek, turn to him the other also. And if someone wants to sue you and take your tunic, let him have your cloak as well. If someone forces you to go one mile, go with him two miles. Give to the one who asks you, and do not turn away from the one who wants to borrow from you.

Matthew 5:38–42

Following Jesus isn't a matter of keeping rules. Jesus takes us beyond rules to a place where we give by instinct, and go beyond what otherwise might have been expected of us. That's the extra mile, and countless Christians have walked it. How about you?

■ Here are some common everyday situations. On the first line write what is normally expected of a neighbour. And on the second, what it might mean to 'go the extra mile'...

A new family moves in next door

The old lady across the road breaks her leg

A member of your church is struggling financially

A mother of three pre-school children is taken into hospital

A real-life situation you face now...

Pray:

Jesus, you keep challenging me. Go on changing me, too. Help me to respond to your great love for me. And take me to the place where I give by instinct. Amen.

HI HO!
HI HO!
IT'S OFF TO
WORK I GO!

JERUSALEM
7
MILES

27

11 *Pray for healing*

At our weekly Bible study group, Sharon was worried: 'I've got to go and see the doctor tomorrow. There's this lump on my left breast.' She asked us to pray for her, so we did. We asked God to heal her.

But I don't think anyone was prepared for the news she brought the following week: 'Hey! You know that lump you prayed about? When I went to the doctor... it had gone! I told him we'd prayed about it, and he was **gobsmacked**.'

Prayer for healing is one way we can show our love for people. If we are truly concerned, then of course we will pray. And not only out of concern, but because Jesus tells us to:

Read:

> When Jesus had called the Twelve together, he gave them power and authority to ... cure diseases, and he sent them out to preach the kingdom of God and to heal the sick ... So they set out and went from village to village, preaching the gospel and healing people everywhere.

Luke 9:1–2, 6

DO YOU WANT TO BE PRAYED FOR PRIVATELY OR ARE YOU ON THE NATIONAL HEALTH?

There's no guarantee that God will always do what we ask. But we know from Jesus that he likes to heal people. So ask God to heal people you know to be poorly—when they're there with you if possible—and see what happens.

In the space below write the names of people you know to be ill...

Now choose one of those people. Make a note of where, when, and with whom you could pray for their healing.

Pray:

Father God, thank you that Jesus healed the sick.
Thank you that he's still doing it today. Give me
love, and faith, and courage. And help me to
pray believing your power to heal. Amen.

12 *Stick at it!*

In the last unit, we saw something remarkable: a group of Christians prayed for their friend, and almost at once she was healed. Let's call that an 'arrow' answer to prayer.

It doesn't always happen like that, though. In God's wisdom, it seems, there are also 'tortoise' answers. These set off at the same time as the arrows but take months or even years to arrive.

WE'LL BE HANGING HERE FOREVER

God has many things to teach us. He uses many ways to do it. If his answer arrives like an arrow, we learn about his power and involvement with the world. If it sets off like a tortoise, we learn lessons of stickability and patience. Jesus approves of such patience, and urges his followers to show it in their prayer lives ...

Read:

- JUST HAVE PATIENCE -

Jesus ... said: 'In a certain town there was a judge who neither feared God nor cared about men. And there was a widow in that town who kept coming to him with the plea, "Grant me justice against my adversary."
For some time he refused. But finally he said to himself, "Even though I don't fear God or care about men, yet because this widow keeps bothering me, I will see that she gets justice, so that she won't eventually wear me out with her coming!" And the Lord said, 'Listen to what the unjust judge says. And will not God bring about justice for his chosen ones, who cry out to him day and night? I tell you, he will see that they get justice, and quickly.'

Luke 18:1–8

'Arrow' answers arrive immediately and teach us about God's power. 'Tortoise' answers set off slowly and teach us about stickability. I wonder how many Christians have given up over the years, and how many 'tortoises' hang motionless in mid-air because people have given up praying for them to arrive?

Write the date in the box provided. Then make a note of three things you'd like to pray faithfully for...

Date: [ ]

		→→→→→
1.		
2.		
3.		

When you've worked to the end of the book, find this unit again. If what you're praying for has happened, tick the 'arrow' column. If it hasn't, tick the 'tortoise'... and stick at it!

Pray:

Father, so many things are 'instant' today. But you've got lessons for me in things I have to wait for. Help me to stick at it, and faithfully to pray 'your kingdom come'. Amen.

LOOKS LIKE THEY'VE FORGOTTEN ME!

Headlines

In this box write your headline from Section One (see page 16)

1.

Now look back at Section Two. What **one thing** would you like to work on to help you **live like Jesus**? Write it in one sentence in this box . . .

2.

Section Three: Changing the World

The purpose of God's kingdom is to change the world (unit 13). Jesus calls us to serve the poor (14) which is the same as serving **him** (15). We share Jesus' work of setting the oppressed free (16) and to do that we need to be involved in politics (17).

13 God's yeast

Take 450g of plain flour. Add a pinch of salt. Mix in 300ml of warm water. And what have you got? A heavy, dead lump of goo. Not much use to anybody, unless you've run out of wallpaper paste.

But add 15g of yeast, and the whole thing springs to life! The yeast works through the dough, pocketing it with air bubbles. The mixture swells and rises. It becomes springy and elastic. It's alive! It has a mind of its own. And once you've baked it you have bread: the staff of life across the world.

Yeast has the power to **change** dough completely. So it's no surprise when Jesus uses it as a picture of his work . . .

Read:

The kingdom of heaven is like yeast that a woman took and mixed into a large amount of flour until it worked all through the dough.

Matthew 13:33

Just as yeast works through a dead lump of dough and brings it to life, so the effect of God's kingdom is to change the world. But God's kingdom can only work through people. Our calling is to act as God's yeast. To work for **life** in his world. And to change it for the better.

■ Let's actually *see* what Jesus is on about ...

You will need:
450g/1lb plain white flour
15ml/1tsp salt
15g/½oz fresh yeast
5ml/1tsp sugar
300ml/10floz lukewarm water

To make:
1 Sieve the flour and salt into a warm bowl.
2 Cream the yeast with the sugar and *most of the liquid.*
3 Make a well in the centre of the flour, pour in the yeast liquid and sprinkle a little flour on top.
4 Cover the bowl with a clean cloth and leave for about 20 minutes, until the surface is covered with bubbles.
5 Mix the liquid with the flour, if too dry add sufficient lukewarm water to give an elastic dough.
6 Turn out of the bowl on to a floured board and knead until smooth.
7 Put back into the bowl and cover with a cloth and leave to rise until almost double the original size.

Now take the bowl and put it in front of you. See what a change the yeast has made. Prod the dough: it's springy. Pull it: it's stretchy.

Think about what you've read and about what you've seen. Then write the name of your town in the blank, and complete the sentence ...

For me to be God's yeast in . . . . means . . . .

. . . .

Then with your eyes open, pray this prayer. . .

Pray:
Lord Jesus, just as the yeast has worked through this dough, send me out into your world to change it. Work through me. And may I play my part, however small, to make your world more as you would wish it. Amen.

14 *Rich man, poor man*

As I write these words, and as you read them, there are people dying of hunger. 24 every minute. 1,440 every hour. 35,000 every day. 18 million every year.

As I write these words, and as you read them, there are people walking miles to fetch water. More than likely it's dirty and diseased. There are doctors watching patients die of diseases they could easily cure. If only they had the medicines.

We know all about these people. They live thousands of miles away but our TV screens have put them on our doorstep, like the beggar in Jesus' parable.

Read:

> *There was a rich man who was dressed in purple and fine linen and lived in luxury every day. At his gate was laid a beggar named Lazarus, covered with sores and longing to eat what fell from the rich man's table. Even the dogs came and licked his sores.*
>
> **Luke 16:19–21**

Jesus goes on to tell how both men died. The beggar was taken to heaven. The rich man to the other place. But Jesus didn't just tell this story to describe life after death. He told this story to make us think about our lives **before** death, our lives **now**. He wants to ask us one direct question: what are **you** doing about the poor?

■ We will think later on (unit 28) about giving to the poor. For the time being, let's think about speaking up for them. This country is relatively very well off. If *you* don't tell your leaders to share that wealth better, who will?

So write a short letter, addressed to The Minister for Overseas Development, Overseas Development Administration, 94 Victoria Street, London, SW1E 5JL

Tell the minister that you would like more of this country's wealth to be spent on the poorest of the earth. And before you post it, pray this prayer over your letter . . .

Pray:

Lord Jesus who spoke for the poor, I dedicate this letter to you. May it reach its goal, be read and acted upon. And make this not an empty gesture from me, but the start of a new concern for the starving, the weak, and the powerless. Amen.

15 | *You did it for me*

What if it was **Jesus** who was starving to death? Or walking miles to collect drinking water? Or living in a sewage pipe in the shanty towns of Latin America?

What if it were **Jesus** sitting in a refugee camp with only one set of clothes? Or waiting in a Sudanese hospital for essential drugs? Or crammed into an overcrowded prison cell?

The thing is, it **is** Jesus . . .

Read:

The King will say to those on his right, 'Come, you who are blessed by my Father; take your inheritance . . . For I was hungry and you gave me something to eat, I was thirsty and you gave me something to drink, I was a stranger and you invited me in, I needed clothes and you clothed me, I was sick and you looked after me, I was in prison and you came to visit me.' Then the righteous will answer him, 'Lord, when did we see you hungry and feed you, or thirsty and give you something to drink? When did we see you a stranger and invite you in, or needing clothes and clothe you? When did we see you sick or in prison and go to visit you?' The King will reply, 'I tell you the truth, whatever you did for one of the least of these brothers of mine, you did for me.'

Matthew 25:34–40

Jesus is still around us all the time. He's present in the lives of each person trapped at the bottom of the pile. **He's** the one who cries out to us for food, clean water and shelter. Shall we shrug him off? Or *give him something to eat?*

Here are the addresses of organizations dedicated to serving Jesus in the poorest of the world. Tick the box of an organization you'd like to know more about, and write off for more details...

Serving the...

☐ *STARVING*
   Christian Aid: PO Box 100, London, SE1 7RT

☐ *THIRSTY*
   UNICEF: 55 Lincoln's Inn Fields, London, WC2A 3NB

☐ *HOMELESS*
   Shelter: 88 Old St, London EC1V 9HU

☐ *REFUGEE*
   Save the Children: 17 Grove Lane, London, SE5 8RD

☐ *SICK*
   The Leprosy Mission: Goldhay Way, Orton
   Goldhay, Peterborough, Cambs, PE2 0GZ

☐ *PRISONER*
   The Prison Fellowship: PO Box 945, Chelmsford, Essex, CM2 7PX

Pray:

I saw you on the news tonight,
Jesus. You were huddled at the
feeding station waiting for rice.
I don't want to you to go
through that agony, Jesus. So I
won't pass by on the other side.
I'll do all I can to help you.
Amen.

16 *Set them free!*

She is four years old. She works six days a week. Her working day lasts eighteen hours. She works in a coal mine, pulling trucks full of coal through tunnels too low for the horses.

The place is Lancashire, England. The date: early 1800s. She is only one of many thousands of children working inhuman hours in the factories and mine

Her plight was noticed by a Christian Member of Parliament: Lord Shaftesbury, the *poor man's earl*. Shaftesbury brought to the House of Commons bill after bill to protect children in the workplace. Children today still have cause to thank him.

In an important respect, Lord Shaftesbury was someone who lived like Jesus. For Jesus applied to himself these words from the prophet Isaiah...

Read:

> *The Spirit of the Lord is on me, because he has anointed me to preach good news to the poor. He has sent me to proclaim freedom for the prisoners and recovery of sight for the blind, to release the oppressed, to proclaim the year of the Lord's favour.*

> *Luke 4:18–19*

Jesus saw it as his work to *release the oppressed*. Down the years his followers have joined him. Lord Shaftesbury is only one well-known example. There are many more.

There are still oppressed people today, of course. Men, women and children working inhuman hours for a pittance. People imprisoned for their beliefs. Victims of torture.

Let's join with Jesus, and play our part to *set them free*.

40

■ Here's a list of qualities shown by a Christian campaigner like Lord Shaftesbury. Which of them apply to you?

	✓ or ✗
He was a Christian	
He knew that Christianity and politics are linked	
He was aware of oppressed people	
He actually did something about them	
He was prepared to use politics to set them free	

Now write here the name of a group of people you know to be *oppressed* . . .

Now write here the name of a group of people you know to be

And make a note of anything you could do to help *set them free* . . .

Pray:

Lord Jesus, I'm only me. There's a limit to what I can do. But I know that the greatest fool is the one who did nothing because he could only do a little. So let me join in your work of releasing the oppressed. Together we can set them free. Amen.

17 | *The Christian and politics*

Jesus' enemies held the Roman coin before him. 'Tell us what you think,' they said. 'Should we pay taxes to Rome or not?'

They had him this time. It was the perfect trap. If he said 'No. Don't pay your taxes,' they could hand him over to the Romans as a trouble-maker. If he said 'Yes, pay them,' he would anger many Jews, who hated being ruled from Rome.

Jesus recognized the trap. He asked to see the coin. This is what happened next . . .

Read:

> He asked them, 'Whose portrait is this? And whose inscription?' 'Caesar's,' they replied. Then he said to them, 'Give to Caesar what is Caesar's, and to God what is God's.' When they heard this they were amazed. So they left him and went away.
>
> *Matthew 22:20–22*

Jesus' reply has been misunderstood. Some people think he meant 'keep out of politics and get on with the business of being a Christian.' But given all we've seen in Section Three that can't be right. For politics is the machinery by which we change the world.

Jesus did not mean by this remark to keep religion and politics apart. He meant that Christians should do all in their power to help the state *(Give to Caesar what is Caesar's . . .)* But when the state demands something against the will of God, Christians should obey God not the government *(Give . . . to God what is God's.).*

There is a rich tradition of Christian contribution to the life of the state.

There is a rich tradition of peaceful Christian protest. Let's join in both. And change the world.

■ Here's a sliding scale of involvement in politics. How far would you go up it? Start at the bottom and draw a line up to where you would draw the line . . .

Standing for election as a Member of Parliament
Standing for election as a local councillor
Joining the party which, for you, best represents Christian values
Taking symbolic action to bring a cause to public attention (e.g. sleeping in a cardboard box at the railway station)
Getting up a petition about an issue to give to your MP
Writing to your MP about an issue
Writing to the paper about an issue
Voting for the party which, for you, best represents Christian values

Now make a note of *one piece* of political action which you will take as a result of reading this unit . . .

Pray:

Lord Jesus, give me wisdom. Show me where best to give to the life of my country. And prompt me when I need to speak out for you. Amen.

Headlines

In these boxes write your headlines from Sections One and Two (see page 32)

```
┌─────────────────────────────────────────┐
│ 1.                                        │
│                                           │
│                                           │
└─────────────────────────────────────────┘
```

```
┌─────────────────────────────────────────┐
│ 2.                                        │
│                                           │
│                                           │
└─────────────────────────────────────────┘
```

Now look back at Section Three. What **one thing** would you like to work on to help you **live like Jesus**? Write it in one sentence in this box...

```
┌─────────────────────────────────────────┐
│ 3.                                        │
│                                           │
│                                           │
└─────────────────────────────────────────┘
```

Section Four: Inside Out

To Jesus, what we're like on the inside is more important than what we're like on the outside (unit 18). From the inside come resentment (19), criticism (20), unforgiveness (21) and lust (22). There's no point pretending anyway, because what we're like on the inside will always show itself in the things that we say (23).

18 *Whitewashed tombs*

My mother once had a nasty surprise. She opened a tin of pineapple chunks for pudding. But there was no pineapple inside. The tin was filled with the remains of a snake. It must have fallen into the canning machine. Not a pretty sight.

That tin of pineapple is a parable about us. All too often we can look very appealing on the outside. What's inside, though, is often very different...

Read:

Woe to you, teachers of the law and Pharisees, you hypocrites! You clean the outside of the cup and dish, but inside they are full of greed and self-indulgence. Blind Pharisee! First clean the inside of the cup and dish, and then the outside also will be clean.
Woe to you, teachers of the law and Pharisees, you hypocrites! You are like whitewashed tombs, which look beautiful on the outside but on the inside are full of dead men's bones and everything unclean. In the same way, on the outside you appear to people as righteous but on the inside you are full of hypocrisy and wickedness.

Matthew 23:25–28

Jesus didn't mince his words with people who pretend to be something they're not. But don't be fooled. This is about you and me as well. God knows everything about us. He sees us working hard on our outward appearance. But to him it matters more what we're like on the inside.

How much time do you spend each week working on your outward appearance? And how much on what you're like inside? Log the amount of time against each item. Then add up your totals...

Outside		Inside	
How much time do I spend		How much time do I spend	
In the bath/shower?		In prayer?	
Shaving/Doing make-up?		Worshipping God?	
Ironing/Polishing shoes?		Reading the Bible?	
Clothes shopping?		In silence?	
Total		Total	

Do you spend more time working on your outside than your inside? What can you do to right the balance? Write some notes in this box...

Pray:

Father, please fill me with your Spirit today. Grow in me your love, your joy and your peace. Help me to know kindness, goodness and faithfulness. And give me gentleness and self-control. Make me clean on the inside, that I may live for you. Amen.

19 *Be reconciled!*

The day after I became a priest I had an argument with my wife. It was something and nothing, no doubt. But I was convinced that I was in the right, and disappeared up the road in an exhaust puff of righteous indignation.

The task in hand was to take Holy Communion to the elderly of the parish. The set Bible passage for the day read as follows...

Read:

> If you are offering your gift at the altar and there remember that your brother has something against you, leave your gift there in front of the altar. First go and be reconciled to your brother; then come and offer your gift.
>
> *Matthew 5:23–24*

I read it aloud at the first house and felt uncomfortable. I read it aloud at the second and felt ashamed. I read it aloud at the third house and had no option. I **had** to go home and sort things out before going any further.

'Quite right', says the Master. It matters to Jesus how we treat each other. There is no difference in his eyes between murder and the anger which causes it. So he says in effect, 'if one of your relationships is wrong, don't worship God till you've sorted it out.' *Be reconciled ... then come and offer your gift.*

48

■ Who do *you* need to be reconciled to? Write their initials in the box. Then on the postcard write something of what you'd want to say.

Now make a note of when and where you'd be able to say that in person.

Pray:

This one might be tricky, Lord. But I know that what you're calling me to do is right. So give me courage and forgiveness. And help me to be reconciled. Amen.

20 *Mind the plank!*

I was driving home one dark night. Suddenly I made out two teenagers cycling the other way. I nearly didn't see them, because neither of them had lights.

This brought out the 'good citizen' in me, and as they approached I flashed my headlights four or five times with full beam. As we passed they gave me that kind of 'who does he think he is?' look. I drove on with that warm glow of having done my bit, but tutting at the cockiness of youth.

But with a jolt, I realized: my lights weren't on either. I was much more of a public hazard than they were! I blushed hot as I switched them on.

The way some people have of charging round the world criticizing everyone but themselves lies behind one of Jesus' best known word-cartoons . . .

Read:

> *Why do you look at the speck of sawdust in your brother's eye and pay no attention to the plank in your own eye? How can you say to your brother, 'Let me take the speck out of your eye', when all the time there is a plank in your own eye? You hypocrite, first take the plank out of your own eye, and then you will see clearly to remove the speck from your brother's eye.*
>
> **Matthew 7:3–5**

Criticizing anybody but ourselves is a common problem. It's our first instinct when something goes wrong. Blame somebody else!

Jesus turns that habit on its head. He says, in effect, 'criticize yourself first! If something is wrong with the world around you, look in the mirror. **You** change first, and then you might be able to change others.'

HANG ON! YOU'VE GOT A SPECK IN YOUR EYE!

■ Is there a plank in *your* eye? Test yourself on this questionnaire and find out. Read each statement carefully. Then mark on the 0–10 scale how much it applies to you...

I don't like moody people, but when I'm in a bad mood myself I take it out on other people

0   1   2   3   4   5   6   7   8   9   10

I blame the government about the starving people but don't do anything for them myself

0   1   2   3   4   5   6   7   8   9   10

I like people to apologize to me but never apologize myself

0   1   2   3   4   5   6   7   8   9   10

I wait for other people to encourage me rather than looking for people to encourage

0   1   2   3   4   5   6   7   8   9   10

When something goes wrong my first instinct is to blame somebody else rather than myself

0   1   2   3   4   5   6   7   8   9   10

Now add up your score. Write it in the box.

How did you get on? If your score is above 25 ... mind out! You've got a plank in your eye and could cause untold damage. Get it seen to, quick!

Pray:

Dear carpenter Jesus, in your love please help me. There's a great big plank in my eye. I'm always finding fault with others, but rarely with myself. Give me a clear eye to see my own faults, and the good in other people. Amen.

51

21 *Father, forgive them!*

The crematorium service had just started when a woman crept into the chapel. Just before the service ended she crept out again. The chapel warden asked her what was going on. It turned out that the woman had had a child before she was married. Her father had completely cut her off. He never forgave her. Now, decades later, she was creeping guiltily to his funeral.

Such a lack of forgiveness, stretched out over a lifetime, is difficult to understand. We can only imagine the effect it had on the daughter, and the father who cut her off.

It's an extreme example, of course. But many of us prefer to harbour grudges than to forgive people who hurt us. It's not an option for the disciple of Jesus

Read:

> *Then Peter came to Jesus and asked, 'Lord, how many times shall I forgive my brother when he sins against me? Up to seven times?' Jesus answered, 'I tell you, not seven times, but seventy-seven times.'*
>
> **Matthew 18:21–22**

Jesus goes on to tell a story about a king who cancelled the enormous debt of his servant. The king of course stands for God. He forgives us perfectly. Our master calls us to forgive those around us in the same way.

Empty words? With Jesus, never. When Roman soldiers were nailing him to the cross he cried out 'Father, forgive them! They don't know what they're doing.'

■ Jesus calls us to forgive not simply because we have been forgiven. He knows that to harbour resentment is bad for us. By forgiving we release that inner hurt.

Who do you need to forgive? Write their initials in the space in the prayer.

Now ask yourself: 'can I pray this prayer?'...

Father God, I forgive........ I release to you all the anger I feel towards him/her. Help me sincerely to want what is best for him/her. And help me to forget it ever happened. Amen.

If you can, then pray the prayer out loud in a private place. If you can't then don't. God doesn't want you to pretend. Instead, write the initials in this second prayer...

Father, I want to forgive........ But I can't. Please help me to see him/her as you see him/her. And to forgive him/her sincerely, from my heart. Amen.

Pray this second prayer as whole-heartedly as you can. And when you feel you can go back to the first prayer, do so.

Pray:

Dear God, thank you that you forgive me perfectly every time I fail. Thank you that I don't have to be perfect to be yours. Help me to live like Jesus, and to forgive the people who hurt me. Amen.

The adultery of the heart

I'd spent the whole day in a monastery, for heaven's sake! I was filled with holy thoughts. But it still happened. I turned left out of the monastery car park and saw a beautiful girl waiting for the bus. The holy thoughts went for a burton! Woops! Sorry, Lord!

A daydream? Appreciating the beauty of God's creation? Jesus has a more direct term for it. He calls it 'adultery' . . .

Read:

> *You have heard that it was said 'Do not commit adultery.' But I tell you that anyone who looks at a woman lustfully has already committed adultery with her in his heart.*

Matthew 5:27–28

Adultery is a destructive force. It pulls whole families apart. That's why from the earliest times it's been outlawed. But Jesus goes further. He says that adultery is something that happens in the mind. We take God's good gift of love and twist it into lust. We turn **people** into **sex objects**.

That's what I was doing on the road home from the monastery. It wasn't wrong to appreciate the girl's beauty. The problem came when appreciation turned to fantasy: when a thought that should instantly have been kicked out was given a warm welcome and room to grow. Forgive me, Lord.

■ I've been honest in this unit. Now it's your turn. After each statement, mark in your mind, or on the 0–10 scale, how much it applies to you...

I sometimes entertain sexual temptation in my head

| 0 | 1 | 2 | 3 | 4 | 5 | 6 | 7 | 8 | 9 | 10 |

I sometimes deliberately flirt with other people

| 0 | 1 | 2 | 3 | 4 | 5 | 6 | 7 | 8 | 9 | 10 |

I sometimes watch blue videos

| 0 | 1 | 2 | 3 | 4 | 5 | 6 | 7 | 8 | 9 | 10 |

I sometimes lie to myself about what I've been doing

| 0 | 1 | 2 | 3 | 4 | 5 | 6 | 7 | 8 | 9 | 10 |

I sometimes pretend with God that nothing's happened

| 0 | 1 | 2 | 3 | 4 | 5 | 6 | 7 | 8 | 9 | 10 |

I sometimes read pornographic magazines

| 0 | 1 | 2 | 3 | 4 | 5 | 6 | 7 | 8 | 9 | 10 |

I sometimes view certain friends as sex objects

| 0 | 1 | 2 | 3 | 4 | 5 | 6 | 7 | 8 | 9 | 10 |

And don't forget: Sex is a good gift of God. It's something to be celebrated! But the maker's advice is to contain his good gift within marriage.

And don't forget either: That there are other ways apart from sex of expressing your sexuality.

Pray:

Father, thank you that in your love you gave us sex. Forgive me for times I've spoilt your gift. And help me to value the people around me for who they are. Amen.

23 | *The overflow*

He dreamt an angel took him by the hand and led him into a small room. On the desk stood a TV screen linked to a computer. 'You've been alive for forty-six years', said the angel. 'Let's check your use of words, and see what effect they've had on other people.'

The angel pressed a button. There before him on the screen was displayed his total use of words throughout his life. They were recorded under various headings. Great long bars for 'Gossip' and 'Lies'. Short blips for 'Encouragement' and 'Peace-Making'.

After a pause to let it sink in, the angel spoke again. 'Not very good, is it?' His heart sank as he nodded. 'What do you want to do about it?' 'I'd like to go back and start again.'

No sooner were the words out of his mouth than he woke up at home in bed. He found the old family Bible, and flipping through it chanced upon these words of Jesus . . .

Read:

> *Out of the overflow of the heart the mouth speaks. The good man brings good things out of the good stored up in him, and the evil man brings evil things out of the evil stored up in him.*
> *But I tell you that men will have to give account on the day of judgment for every careless word they have spoken. For by your words you will be acquitted, and by your words you will be condemned.*
>
> *Matthew 12:34–37*

The words we say tell us something very important about the people we are. The good stuff comes from the good within us. The evil stuff, says Jesus, comes from inside us too: we can't pretend it doesn't.

We have a limited amount of time on this planet. There is a limit to the number of words we can speak. It's up to us to use those words for good, and not for evil.

Hidden in the word square are ten ways we can use words. Some are good, others not. As you find each one, list it in the appropriate box...

C	G	T	H	A	B	U	S	E
T	R	O	F	M	O	C	U	G
C	A	I	S	D	G	R	Y	A
N	D	P	T	R	U	H	D	R
S	R	C	R	I	L	E	N	U
H	A	A	W	A	C	T	E	O
N	E	O	W	S	I	I	N	C
D	W	G	L	C	L	S	Z	N
T	S	E	T	O	R	P	E	E

Protest
Encourage
Warn
Praise
Abuse
Swear
Lie
Criticize
Comfort
Hurt

Good	*Evil*

Now look at the words in your 'good' box. Circle the use of words you'd most like to improve on. Then look at the words in your 'evil' box. Which do you do most? Circle it, and pray for God to help you do better.

Pray:

Father, thank you for the gift of words. I'm sorry for the times I've used them to hurt other people. Help me to use them to build up those around me. Amen.

Headlines

In these boxes write your headlines from Sections One to Three (see page 44)

> 1.

> 2.

> 3.

Now look back at Section Four. What **one thing** would you like to work on to help you **live like Jesus**? Write it in one sentence in this box...

> 4.

Section Five: Your Money and Your Life

We are called to imitate the generosity of God (unit 24) by giving to others (25). The rich man in Jesus' story was a fool because he hoarded money to himself (26) when he could have been *rich towards God* (27). Jesus calls us to a simple lifestyle (28), a lifestyle of complete trust in God (29).

24 | *Give generously*

It happened while I was up to my waist in brambles. One large plastic pot already full. Another filling quickly. Suddenly I saw them all: tens, hundreds, thousands of blackberries, burdening the bush with fruit. I knew they were there, of course. Now I just stood and gawped. With new eyes I saw the amazing generosity of nature. And saw too a reflection of our good and generous God—who gives us far more than we really need.

According to Jesus, we're to take our cue from this generous God:

Read:

> *Give, and it will be given to you. A good measure, pressed down, shaken together, and running over, will be poured into your lap. For with the measure you use, it will be measured to you.*

Luke 6:38

Alongside our generous God, most of us are unbelievably mean. Not just with our money. With our time and homes as well. But listen to Jesus' rule: God will use the measure you choose. If you give with a teaspoon, you'll get a teaspoon back. If you use a ladle, you'll get that instead.

And if you think about it, that's true. Mean people always seem to be miserable, and penny-pinching. It's warm, open-hearted, generous people who get the most out of life.

So look at the table opposite. If you give a teaspoonful of your time to other people, tick that column. If it's a ladle, tick that. And so on, down the list ...

WHAT'S GOD EVER DONE FOR ME?

What measure do I use...

	teaspoon	tablespoon	ladle
In the amount of time I give to other people?			
In the way I open my home to visitors?			
In getting alongside the lonely?			
In the words I use to encourage others?			
In forgiving people who hurt me?			
In helping the poor?			
In forming my first impressions of people?			

Now choose a subject for which you gave yourself a teaspoon. In the space provided, make a note of action you can take to make it a tablespoon.

Pray:

Father, thank you for the rich world you made. Help me to be like you: generous, kind, and open-hearted. Amen.

25 Secret giving

Joan is a single parent. She suffers from arthritis in her hands, yet had no washing machine. She did all the family's washing by hand. Wash day was not something Joan looked forward to.

When a group from a local church met Joan, they went into action. One family took in her washing for a couple of weeks. An appeal for a washing machine was placed in the weekly news sheet. Another family answered it. Within days the machine had been delivered, plumbed in and was working.

Jesus takes it for granted that his followers will want to give. Not because they're forced to. Not because of set religious rules. Just because they're like that. Their love overflows in giving...

Read:

> *When you give to the needy, do not announce it with trumpets, as the hypocrites do in the synagogues and on the streets, to be honoured by men ... But when you give to the needy, do not let your left hand know what your right hand is doing, so that your giving may be in secret. Then your Father, who sees what is done in secret, will reward you.*
>
> *Matthew 6:2–4*

YOU TRY DELIVERING A WASHING MACHINE QUIETLY!

According to Jesus, we're to give. Moreover we're to give in secret, so that we hide it even from ourselves. But what have **we** got to give? Perhaps more than we think...

Take a look at the table below. Tick the items that apply to you, then make a note of how you could use them to help others ...

I've got ...	✓	
More money than I need		
Time on my hands		
A car		
More clothes than I need		
Spare baby equipment		
Tools I never use		

Pray:

Father, you have given me so much. I want to give to others gladly, generously, and in secret. Help me to catch the Jesus bug: help me to give without thinking. Amen.

26 | *The rich fool*

Jesus of Nazareth was a wandering teacher. He had no home. He had very few possessions. He sometimes depended on the generosity of others. Yet in his teaching you will find no shred of envy towards the rich. Quite the reverse. Jesus felt sorry for most rich people. Their wealth brought more worry. They often couldn't see beyond their money. So all too often they completely missed the point. Like the central character in this short, haunting parable...

Read:

The ground of a certain rich man produced a good crop. He thought to himself, 'What shall I do? I have no place to store my crops.' Then he said, 'This is what I'll do. I will tear down my barns and build bigger ones, and there I will store all my grain and my goods. And I'll say to myself, "You have plenty of good things laid up for many years. Take life easy; eat, drink and be merry."' But God said to him, 'You fool! This very night your life will be demanded from you. Then who will get what you have prepared for yourself?'
This is how it will be with anyone who stores up things for himself but is not rich towards God.

Luke 12:16–21

The rich man was a fool because he'd got his priorities completely wrong. He'd devoted his life to getting rich for himself, when the point is to be *rich towards God*. Then came his heart attack, or his brain haemorrhage, and his riches meant nothing. His life had stood for selfishness and greed. Now it was over it stood for nothing. *'You fool!'*

So that we don't end up in the same boat, here's a little priority test. The more honest you can be with yourself, the better. Look at the list of priorities, and in the first column rank them in order as they are now...

	Now	6 months
The way I look		
The kind of car I drive		
My relationship with my family		
Popularity		
Making money		
My relationship with God		
My career prospects		
The kind of house I live in		
Serving other people		
My leisure interests (sport etc)		

Now look at your full order of priorities. Are you happy with them? If not, re-order them in the second column for where you'd like to be in six months' time.

Now write down *one thing* you need to do to take a step nearer your second column.

Pray:

Thank you, Father, for the gift of life. Help me not to miss the point. Help me take the action I need to make my life richer towards you. Amen.

65

27 | *Treasure in heaven*

Strange to say it, but one of the richest people I ever met had next to nothing. She was called Peg, and she was a cleaning lady at my college. Every morning she would get up at four and provide for her bed-ridden husband. Then came the five mile walk to work.

Peg was an Irish Catholic, and her little cubby-hole was her shrine. She had the Sacred Heart on the mantelpiece, and there, during tea-breaks, she would say her rosary for every student on the corridor. When I bumped into her on the landing I'd be swept into a waltz by her ancient, wiry arms.

Peg hardly ever had two pennies to rub together. But she was rich beyond my wildest dreams, for she had learnt the Jesus secret of riches...

Read:

> Do not store up for yourselves treasures on earth, where moth and rust
> destroy, and where thieves break in and steal. But store up for yourselves
> treasures in heaven, where moth and rust do not destroy, and where thieves
> do not break in and steal. For where your treasure is, there your heart will be
> also.
>
> **Matthew 6:19–21**

In Peg's case, Jesus' words had a deeper meaning. For she was murdered in a city-centre public toilet by a thief who stole what little earthly treasure she had. But no-one could touch the real source of her treasure. For it was kept for her in heaven by Jesus. There she enjoys it today.

■ In the space provided, make a list of all the ways you can think of to *store up treasure in heaven* ...

Now, choosing one of the things you've listed, complete the following sentence ...

I resolve to store up treasure in heaven by ....

....

....

Pray:

Father, there's more to life than money. And a different kind of richness. Help me to ignore the pressures of the world around me, and to become rich on the inside. Amen.

28 | *Give to the poor*

He was born in 1181, the son of a rich merchant. After a serious illness, restless with his wealthy lifestyle, he decided to give himself to the service of the poor. He once changed places with a beggar. The experience of being penniless deeply affected him.

We know him as St Francis. One day in 1208 he heard the call of Jesus to leave everything and spread the good news. His generosity and simple faith soon drew a following. And down the years his movement, the Franciscans, has been used by God to touch many, many people.

Francis heard the call of Jesus. He responded, unlike the rich young man Mark tells us about . . .

Read:

As Jesus started on his way, a man ran up to him and fell on his knees before him. 'Good teacher,' he asked, 'what must I do to inherit eternal life?' . . .
Jesus looked at him and loved him. 'One thing you lack,' he said. 'Go, sell everything you have and give to the poor, and you will have treasure in heaven. Then come, follow me.' At this the man's face fell. He went away sad, because he had great wealth.

Mark 10:17–22

Let's be clear about this: we cannot buy our way into God's favour. He loves us perfectly anyway. But down the years the call of Jesus to sell everything has been dulled. We like to think he just meant that particular young man. And our lifestyle remains almost identical with those around us. We ought to think again, and take steps towards a simpler lifestyle. Let's live simply, so that others may simply live.

In the left hand column, write things that you buy but could do without. In the middle column, estimate how much you would save if you didn't buy them. And in the right hand column write who could benefit from a gift of that money...

	£	

Pray:

Lord, make me an instrument of your peace.
Where there is hatred, let me sow love;
where there is injury, pardon;
where there is doubt, faith;
where there is despair, hope;
where there is darkness, light;
where there is sadness, joy.
Amen.

St Francis of Assisi: 1181–1226

29 *Don't worry!*

Our ageing Triumph car had a service before we set off. After all, we were going to the middle of France and you can't be too careful.

When we collected it the mechanic was his usual cheery self: 'Where are you taking it? France? I wouldn't even take it to Tesco!!'

'Thanks', I said, and climbed in.

'And by the way: go easy on the gears!'

'Why?!'

'Your clutch is almost shot. But it should do you. Have a nice time!'

Have a nice time?! When you're the worrying sort? And hundreds of miles from home in a foreign country? With all your gear and a toddler and a car about to pack in? *Have a nice time*? I worried myself sick for fifteen hundred miles.

But back in Merrie England, with the car still in one piece, I was forced to think. What was the value of all that anxiety? Did my worrying do anything to help the car along the road? Was there any link **at all** between my grey hairs and the gearbox? Of course not, and I heard with new ears these words of the Master...

Read:

Do not worry about your life, what you will eat; or about your body, what you will wear. Life is more than food, and the body more than clothes...
Who of you by worrying can add a single hour to his life? Since you cannot do this very little thing, why do you worry about the rest?

Luke 12:22–26

Jesus' words do not encourage us to a life of reckless stupidity. There are certain things it's very proper to be concerned about. But looking at our stressed-out society Jesus would certainly tell us we worry too much. And he would gently call us towards a life of complete trust in God.

■ **What do you worry about? Circle the issue you worry about most, or add your own in the space provided...**

Where will the money come from?

Will there be a nuclear war?

Will the children settle in a new town?

Will I get cancer one day?

What do other people think about me?

Will the planet survive all our pollution?

Now tell God in your own words about your worry. Then still yourself and listen for a response.

Pray:

God, grant me the serenity to accept the things I cannot change. Courage to change the things I can. And wisdom to know the difference. Amen.

Headlines

In these boxes write your headlines from Section One to Four (see page 58)

1.

2.

3.

4.

Now look back at Section Five. What **one thing** would you like to work on to help you **live like Jesus**? Write it in one sentence in this box . . .

5.

Section Six: Power for Living

Jesus drew strength from his relationship with a loving God (unit 30). His advice is that we do the same (31). God also sends us his Holy Spirit to empower us (32) and refresh us (33). Jesus' promise is that if we keep close to him, we will enjoy a fruitful life (34).

30 *Coming home*

My father-in-law is in the Navy. He can be away at sea for months on end. So we have pictures of him around the house. They remind our children of Grandad, and prompt us to remember times they've spent with him.

Recently he was home on leave, and his car drew up outside our house. They knew exactly who he was and rushed up the drive to meet him: 'Grandad!'

It's one thing to miss someone for six months. The Bible on the other hand says that no-one has *ever* seen God. (John 1:18) But that God, the only Son... has made him known.

Jesus made God known to us in various ways. One of them was very similar to our pictures of Grandad. He told stories that painted word-pictures of God. From them we learn what God is like, and learn to recognize him when we meet him one day.

Perhaps the best known of Jesus' word-pictures of God is that of the father in his story of the prodigal son...

Read:

While he was still a long way off, his father saw him and was filled with compassion for him; he ran to his son, threw his arms around him and kissed him. The son said to him, 'Father, I have sinned against heaven and against you. I am no longer worthy to be called your son.' But the father said to his servants, 'Quick! Bring the best robe and put it on him. Put a ring on his finger and sandals on his feet. Let's have a feast and celebrate. For this son of mine was dead and is alive again; he was lost and is found.' So they began to celebrate.

Luke 15:20–24

This is Jesus' picture of his Father. This is God. Overjoyed when we come home. Truly, genuinely in love with us. This is the Father Jesus loved to be with. The one whose company he sought by withdrawing from the crowd. The one from whom he drew power for living. This section will try to help you do the same.

But first, put yourself into Jesus' story. Take time to be still. Imagine you're the son who left home. You've wasted the family wealth. You don't expect a welcome. But you're going home to ask your Dad if you can be his slave. Picture yourself walking along the road home.

Now imagine the Father has seen you. He runs down the road to meet you. He throws his arms around you. He holds you close. He won't hear of you being a slave but receives you fully back into the family. Take time in the stillness to enjoy God's love.

Pray:

Father God, thank you for your perfect love. Help me to see you as you really are, and to spend time enjoying you. And may I draw from you the same power for living that Jesus knew. Amen.

31 *The secret place*

Every morning the priest saw the farmer make his way into church. Half an hour later he came out again. A quick splash of holy water and he was off, back to the fields.

One day the priest's curiosity got the better of him and he asked, 'what do you **do** in there?' The farmer replied, simply, 'I look at him. He looks at me. And we are happy.'

Time spent alone with God is the Christian's lifeline. If we still ourselves for long enough we will discover how much God loves us. If we do, it will be our joy to return that love. We shall enter the love affair with God that true life is all about.

That was Jesus' experience. He needed to spend time along with his Father. He recommends that we do the same . . .

Read:

> *When you pray, go into your room, close the door and pray to your Father, who is unseen. Then your Father, who sees what is done in secret, will reward you. And when you pray, do not keep on babbling like pagans, for they think they will be heard because of their many words. Do not be like them, for your Father knows what you need before you ask him.*
>
> **Matthew 6:6–8**

The word 'prayer' has had a bad press. It sounds like hard work. It sounds boring. It sounds like something we **ought** to do. But it needn't be any of those things. For the aim of prayer is simply to enjoy being with God. Here are some ideas how that might happen . .

LORD, I'M REALLY WORRIED ABOUT MY DAUGHTER.....

...... I KNOW — SHE'S GOING INTO HOSPITAL TOMORROW, BUT SO AM I..... IN FACT I AM ALREADY THERE.

Listed below are ways we can pray. Plan some time alone with God by choosing items from the list, in any order you like. Write them in the blank table. You don't have to choose all the items: it's like a menu. But once you've planned it, do it. And enjoy being with God...

Look at an object of beauty	
Pray for the needs of others	
Read a passage from the Bible	
Listen to God	
Be still	
Think through the events of yesterday	
Say 'sorry' to God	
Thank God for all he's given me	
Sing to God	
Listen to music	
Ask God to help me	
Pray for the needs of the world	

Pray:

Father, I don't know quite why I draw back from you. You are my life, but there's something in me that keeps me from you. Help me to overcome it and to meet you in the secret place. Amen.

32 *Stay in the city*

Near where I live, high in the Yorkshire Pennines, there is a wind tower. Its tall white shape dominates the landscape. Its three blades gracefully spin, turning wind into power.

But when there is **no** wind? There is no power. No matter how large, graceful or imposing it is. A wind farm is useless without wind. It simply cannot do the job.

Strong wind, and power, have always been closely linked. That's why when God sent his Holy Spirit on the Day of Pentecost the disciples heard *a sound like the blowing of a violent wind.*

The Spirit was sent to equip Christians. To give us the power to do the job. So Jesus told his disciples to do **nothing** until he came . . .

Read:

I am going to send you what my Father has promised; but stay in the city until you have been clothed with power from on high . . . For John baptised with water, but in a few days you will be baptised with the Holy Spirit.

Luke 24:49, Acts 1:5

Living like Jesus is hard, but God doesn't expect us to do it in our own strength. He himself gives us the power, by his Spirit. So let the wind of the Spirit blow through you. Or else your life as a Christian will be as ineffective as a wind farm on a still day.

■ Look back through the book. Which three things that Jesus has called you to are the most difficult for you? Write them in these spaces...

1.	
2.	
3.	

Now read this sentence out loud:

Heavenly Father, I understand that you do not want me to attempt these things in my own strength. I know your Spirit will help me. I want to let him help me.

Pray:

Come, Holy Spirit. Blow the mighty wind of your power into me. Help me to live like Jesus. Amen.

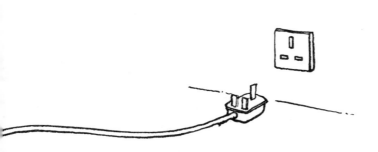

33 *Come and drink*

On the hot, dusty plains of central Spain, water is hard to come by. Supplies are brought in by tanker. At the boarding-house we were allowed one bucket of sandy water a day to wash in.

Going out in the heat of the day was not a good idea. I have never known such thirst. My mouth was soon coated with a thick white cream. Life became a matter of staggering from one cold drink to the next.

In the hot and dusty land where Jesus lived, thirst is also a common experience. But he spoke of a different kind of thirst, a thirst inside . . .

Read:

> *If anyone is thirsty, let him come to me and drink. Whoever believes in me, as Scripture has said, streams of living water will flow from within him. By this he meant the Spirit, whom those who believed in him were later to receive . . .*
>
> ***John 7:37–39***

The thirst that Jesus spoke of cannot be quenched with water. It's a thirst for meaning. For acceptance and love. For the power to live. In short, a thirst for God. But hear again the words of Jesus' invitation: *if anyone is thirsty, let him come to me and drink.*

■ Let's drink from Jesus. Find a comfortable position and take time to be quiet and still. Then write in this box an area of your life where you feel dry and thirsty. (It could be your prayer life. Or a relationship. Or a job you've been asked to do at church. Anything.)

Now either out loud, or in your mind, use this prayer from Psalm 42. Say the prayer at least three times, dwelling on each phrase and what it means . . .

As the deer pants for streams of water,
so my soul pants for you, O God.
My soul thirsts for God, for the living God.
When can I go and meet with God?

Now use your imagination to picture yourself drinking something cool. You could be at a drinking fountain, or stood under a small waterfall, or bursting open an ice-cold can of coke.

Then, remembering that Jesus likens his Spirit to *living water*, pray this prayer . . .

Pray:

Lord Jesus, I am thirsty and I come to you to drink. Flood me with your presence, and give me the power to live. Then help me to come again, and again. Help me to go on drinking from you. Amen.

BUT NOTHING FOR INNER THIRST

34 | *Remain in the vine*

I once walked for miles along a road through a vineyard. I have never seen so much fruit. Perfect soil conditions, healthy vines: hundreds of thousands of grapes.

But take a saw and lop off one of those branches. Cut off from the source of its life it begins to wither instantly. In a couple of days it's only useful for firewood.

Jesus used that picture to help us think about our relationship with him...

Read:

I am the vine; you are the branches. If a man remains in me and I in him, he will bear much fruit; apart from me you can do nothing. If anyone does not remain in me, he is like a branch that is thrown away and withers; such branches are picked up, thrown into the fire and burned. If you remain in me and my words remain in you, ask for whatever you wish and it will be given you. This is to my Father's glory, that you bear much fruit, showing yourselves to be my disciples.

John 15:5–8

In the last unit, we asked the Holy Spirit to help us live the Christian life. But that isn't a one-off. We need to go on being constantly filled and re-filled. That's what Jesus means by *remaining in the vine*—staying close to Jesus and receiving life from his Spirit.

Of course we'll fail from time to time. We'll cut ourselves off from the vine and our life will begin to wither. But it's not the end of the world. There is always forgiveness in God. We can return and begin again. And as we continue *in the vine* a crop of good fruit will slowly, naturally, grow in us, *to the Father's glory*.

Here are five types of 'soil' to help us grow as Christians. Draw a line from the foot of the vine into each 'soil' to show how deep you think your roots are...

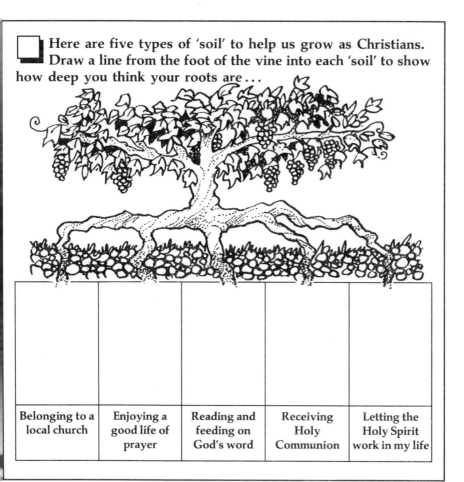

Belonging to a local church	Enjoying a good life of prayer	Reading and feeding on God's word	Receiving Holy Communion	Letting the Holy Spirit work in my life

Pray:

Lord Jesus, it's only as I sink my roots into you that my life will be fruitful. You are the vine. I am your branch. Let your life flow into me: may my life produce a crop of good fruit for you. Amen.

Headlines

In these boxes write your headlines from Sections One to Five (see page 72)

1.

2.

3.

4.

5.

Now look back at Section Six. What **one thing** would you like to work on to help you **live like Jesus**? Write it in one sentence in this box...

6.

Section Seven: Stake Your All

You never know when your End will come (unit 35). So stake your all on God (36) and you will attract others into the kingdom (37).

35 *Keep watch!*

I was pushing my six-week-old son along the pavement in his buggy. Suddenly a lump of masonry, three bricks cemented together, landed on the pavement three feet from his head. The workman looked down and uttered the understatement of the century: 'Oops!'

When I finally got the baby home and lay him in his cot I looked at him with new eyes. We had had a brush with death. A hint of the End. And it had come out of the blue.

Experiences like that can actually help in the long run. They teach us that death can come at any moment. That anything we value can be snatched from us at a moment's notice. So we appreciate them all the more.

Although not speaking about death but about his return, Jesus warns us always to be ready, to keep watch . . .

Read:

> Be dressed ready for service and keep
> your lamps burning, like men waiting for
> their master to return from a wedding
> banquet, so that when he comes and
> knocks they can immediately open the
> door for him. It will be good for those
> servants whose master finds them
> watching when he comes . . . even if
> he comes in the second or third
> watch of the night . . . You
> also must be ready, because
> the Son of Man will come
> at an hour when you do not
> expect him.
>
> Luke 12:35–40

Imagine you were going to die tomorrow. Who would you most want to talk to? Write their name in this space

And what would you want to say? Jot down some notes

Now don't continue the book until you have said those things to that person. You could write, phone, or tell them in person, but make sure you do it! Tick the box when you have, then continue.

Pray:

Dear God, thank you for the gift of life. Help me to live it to the full. And if my End should come today, I gladly place myself into your hands. Amen.

36 Stake your all!

The big heavy winger bore down on me. It was me or nothing. If I didn't tackle him, a try was certain.

As he reached me, his sudden side-step put me on the wrong foot. Not wanting to look too cowardly, I stuck out a half-hearted arm. He brushed past it with disdain, bending it back painfully at the elbow. The try was scored and I was in agony.

You get nothing for half-hearted involvement. That's as true for other walks of life as it is on the rugby field: wishy-washy commitment gets you nowhere.

Jesus knew that. He lived for the Father who had given **everything** to the world he made. He knew that the secret of true life is for us to give our all to him in return . . .

Read:

> The kingdom of heaven is like treasure hidden in a field. When a man found it, he hid it again, and then in his joy went and sold all he had and bought that field. Again, the kingdom of heaven is like a merchant looking for fine pearls. When he found one of great value, he went away and sold everything he had and bought it.
> **Matthew 13:44–46**

Nothing wishy-washy or half-hearted about those responses. Let it be so for you, says Jesus. Stake your all on God. Let your life be a total, joyful celebration of him. Then you'll know what true life really means.

Shade the bar to the extent that each statement is true for you...

My relationship with God is the most important thing in my life

I believe the Christian life should involve joy and celebration

I want to give more of my life to God

Discovering God is like finding a priceless pearl

I believe that Jesus can give me real life.

Pray:

Lord Jesus, thank you for showing me the emptiness of half-hearted commitment. I don't want to be a lukewarm Christian, Lord. I want to stake my all on you. Set me on fire by your Spirit! Amen.

37 | *Send the invitation*

A famous person is to throw a party, and you're invited. In your wildest dreams, who would you want it to be? Write their name here:

_____

Now imagine that person really **has** written to you. Write in one sentence how you feel

_____

Invitations and parties were at the heart of Jesus' life. Time and again he invited his listeners to come and live. And when he wanted a picture of heaven, his mind turned straight away to a great party...

Read:

A certain man was preparing a great banquet and invited many guests. At the time of the banquet he ... ordered his servant, 'Go out quickly into the streets and alleys of the town and bring in the poor, the crippled, the blind and the lame.'
'Sir', the servant said, 'what you ordered has been done, but there is still room.' Then the master told his servant, 'Go out to the roads and country lanes and make them come in, so that my house will be full.'

Luke 14:16–23

Heaven is a great party. And our Father wants his house to be full. So he sends his messengers out with invitations. In all kinds of ways, and at all kinds of times, he invites every human being to the banquet.

If you've accepted his invitation, then become his messenger and take his invitation to others. There are people among your family and friends that God is longing to see at the party. Will you invite them? It is not your responsibility if they do not accept. But God in his love calls you to deliver the invitation.

So think who you could invite. In the boxes write the names of six people among your family, workmates, and friends, who have not yet accepted God's invitation...

Now begin to pray regularly for your six names. And look out for ways you could deliver God's invitation.

Pray:

Heavenly Father, thank you for inviting me to the great banquet of heaven. Gladly I accept. Now make my life, my words, my deeds, into one big invitation. Through your life in me, may many others come and live. Amen.

Headlines

In these boxes write your headlines from Sections One to Six (see page 84)

> 1.

> 2.

> 3.

> 4.

> 5.

> 6.

Now look back at Section Seven. What **one thing** would you like to work on to help you **live like Jesus**? Write it in one sentence in this box...

> 7.

On this page you now have seven Headlines. Areas of your life where you would like the Holy Spirit of Jesus to be at work. Why not write them on a small card and keep it handy? Then wherever you are you can take time out to ask God for the power to **live like Jesus**.

Group study material

For the purposes of the group course, the 37 units have been broken down into groups of 2 or 3. The outline shows which units to group together. This is, of course, a suggested outline. From the outset it is envisaged that group leaders use a certain amount of flexibility.

Each unit has four sections: a 'Thought for the Day' style introduction, a Bible passage, an exercise, and a prayer.

The material works best in a group when read aloud. But be sensitive on this one: not everyone can read aloud, and many people don't enjoy doing so.

Give members plenty of time to fill in the various charts, etc. Then be sure to give people time to buzz their findings in twos or threes before coming together for full group discussion.

Below, you will find **discussion questions** for each unit in the course. These are designed to lead the discussion further, once you've taken initial reactions to the exercise.

The exercises are meant to be as practical as possible. So encourage members of the group to write their targets down. Then look for ways of reminding the group of their own aims.

Week One: Counting the cost (units 1, 2 and 3)

Begin the session by reading out loud the introduction to Section One on page 5. These short intros are designed as sketch maps to help the group see where they're heading.

1 Why do you think people, by and large, decide not to follow the teaching of Jesus? *(unit 1)*

2 Share with the group a story about how you're 'living against the flow'. How can the group help you? *(unit 2)*

3 How has the cost of being a Christian affected you? *(unit 3)*

Week Two: The flavour of God (units 4 and 5)

1 How can your church better spread the flavour of God in your area? *(unit 4)*

2 Why do you think people fill up their spare time with more and more activity? *(unit 5)*

End the session by giving the group time to fill in the 'Headline' section on page 16. Then ask each member to tell their headline to the group, always giving people a chance to 'pass' if it's too personal.

Week Three: The golden rule (units 6, 7 and 8)

Begin by reading the Section Introduction on page 17.

1 What other definitions of love would you want to see added to the list printed in the book? *(unit 6)*

2 Share with the group your experience of someone who was quick at seeing the needs of others. *(unit 7)*

3 What other times can you think of when Jesus showed his love for those around him? *(unit 8)*

Week Four: Love your enemy (units 9 and 10)

1 What would you say to someone who found it impossible to love their enemy? *(unit 9)*
2 Do you think Jesus means that once we've gone the extra mile we've done our duty? Where do you think he wants us to draw the line? *(unit 10)*

Week Five: Pray for healing (units 11 and 12)

1 Why do you think God heals on some occasions, but not on others? *(unit 11)*
2 Share with the group your story of praying at length for something and finally seeing it happen. What lessons do you think God has for us by making us wait? *(unit 12)*
End the session by giving the group time to fill in the 'Headline' section on page 32. Then ask each member to tell their headline to the group, always giving people a chance to 'pass' if it's too personal.

Week Six: God's yeast (units 13, 14 and 15)

Begin by reading the Section Introduction on page 33.
1 Please don't shirk on the bread-making exercise. It's messy; it needs preparation, but please do it! The group needs to see the change the yeast makes to the dough. I would suggest you make your dough, leave it in a warm place, and come back to it after units 14 and 15, ending the session with the exercise at the end of unit 13.
2 Have the materials to hand so that each member of the group can write their letter there and then. Then pile them up and have the group pray the prayer out loud over the pile. If there is a post-box to hand, send a member of the group to post the letters instantly. *(unit 14)*
3 Try to time unit 15 so that the group can watch a news bulletin before you pray the prayer. The news could lead the group into prayer for the wider needs of the world.
4 Now get your dough out of its warm place and complete unit 13.

Week Seven: Set them free! (units 16 and 17)

1 If Lord Shaftesbury were alive today, what sort of things would concern him? What can our church do to bring those things to people's attention? *(unit 16)*
2 Should church leaders be involved in political action? If so, what kind of action should they take? *(unit 17)*
End the session by giving the group time to fill in the 'Headline' section on page 44. Then ask each member to tell their headline to the group, always giving people a chance to 'pass' if it's too personal.

Week Eight: Whitewashed tombs (units 18, 19 and 20)

Begin by reading the Section Introduction on page 45.
1 What ways can you think of, other than those listed in the book, of working on what you're like inside? *(unit 18)*
2 Share with the group a story of when you've been reconciled to somebody. What did it cost? And how did you benefit? *(unit 19)*

3 What if you're prepared to be reconciled, but the other person will have none of it? What's the call of Jesus in that situation? *(unit 19)*
4 What does it mean to 'take the plank out of our own eye?' How do we actually do it? *(unit 20)*

Week Nine: The overflow (units 21, 22 and 23)

1 If somebody really cannot bring themselves to forgive another person, what advice would you give them? *(unit 21)*
2 Be careful to stress here that no-one in the group need put any mark on the 0–10 scale. *(unit 22)*
3 Why do you think God wants sex to be contained within marriage? What would Jesus want to say to somebody in an adulterous relationship? *(unit 22)*
4 Do you agree that 'sticks and stones may break my bones but words will never hurt me?' If not, why not? In the light of your discussion, how should you use words? *(unit 23)*
End the session by giving the group time to fill in the 'Headline' section on page 58. Then ask each member to tell their headline to the group, always giving people a chance to 'pass' if it's too personal.

Week Ten: Give generously (units 24 and 25)

Begin by reading the Section Introduction on page 59.
1 Group game to stress the generosity of God. First player says 'I thank God for runner beans' (for example). Second player says 'I thank God for runner beans and hot buttered toast'. Third player say 'I thank God for runner beans, hot buttered toast, and pepperoni pizza ...' and so on and so on ... *(unit 24)*
2 What does it mean to give in such a way that our left hand does not know what our right hand is doing? Is it possible? *(unit 25)*

Week Eleven: Treasure in heaven (units 26 and 27)

1 Share with the group the story of a time when you've had to re-order your priorities. *(unit 26)*
2 In the group, pool all the ways you can think of to store up treasure in heaven. What does it mean to have your heart in heaven? *(unit 27)*

Week Twelve: Give to the poor (units 28 and 29)

1 What do you think Jesus means when he says 'any of you who does not leave everything he has cannot be my disciple?' (Luke 14:33) How can we best respond to those words in our day? *(unit 28)*
2 Share with the group the story of a time when God has provided for your needs. How did it make you feel about the future? *(unit 29)*
End the session by giving the group time to fill in the 'Headline' section on page 72. Then ask each member to tell their headline to the group, always giving people a chance to 'pass' if it's too personal.

Week Thirteen: Coming home (units 30 and 31)

Begin by reading the Section Introduction on page 73.
1 Unit 30 does not have an exercise, but a meditation. The group leader should talk

the group through the imagination exercise (seek advice if this is new to you). At the end, give the group plenty of time to come round. Then either in buzz groups, or together, share how the exercise made you feel about God, and about yourself.

2 Why do you think some people find it difficult to spend time on their own with God? What advice would you give to someone who did? *(unit 31)*

Week Fourteen: Come and drink (units 32, 33 and 34)

1 What does it mean to do things in our own strength? How can we begin to do things in God's strength? *(unit 32)*

2 For group use, the members should pray the prayer from Psalm 42 silently. The group leader should talk the group through the imagination exercise (see under unit 30). *(unit 33)*

3 Have you ever been 'thirsty inside'? What happened? Have you ever had that thirst quenched? How? *(unit 33)*

4 Have you been able to sink your roots into the life of God? Was Jesus true to his promise that your life would bear much fruit? *(unit 34)*

End the session by giving the group time to fill in the 'Headline' section on page 84. Then ask each member to tell their headline to the group, always giving people a chance to 'pass' if it's too personal.

Week Fifteen: Stake your all! (units 35, 36 and 37)

Begin by reading the Section Introduction on page 85.

1 What are the benefits of 'always being ready for the master'? *(unit 35)*

2 How can we stake our all on God without becoming 'too heavenly minded to be of any earthly use'? *(unit 36)*

3 How do you react to the word 'evangelism'? Is your church an inviting place? If not, what could your group do to make it more so? *(unit 37)*

End the session by giving the group time to fill in the 'Headline' section on page 92. Then ask each member to tell their headline to the group, always giving people a chance to 'pass' if it's too personal.

Then give each member of the group time to write their headlines on a small card. Then each person could share their list of seven, with the same 'pass' rule applying. End the course by breaking into small groups to pray.